Healthy & Light
contents

3

17

47

D1275931

Meredith BOOKS

Des Moines, Iowa

Copyright © 2008 Meredith Corporation
First Edition. Printed in China.
Excerpted from *Better Homes and Gardens® Light & Luscious*, 2004.
ISBN: 978-0-696-24086-7

easy chicken & turkey

chicken, bean, and tomato stir-fry

When it comes to cooking light meals, think poultry. From stir-fries to skillet dishes to pizza, this chapter offers enticing ways to fix chicken or turkey.

chicken, bean, and tomato stir-fry *(see photo, opposite)*

Chinese long beans are one of the stars of Asian stir-fries. These dark green, pencil-thin legumes average 18 inches of crunchy flavor. Look for them in Asian food markets or supermarkets.
Makes 2 servings

- 3 oz. dried wide rice noodles or egg noodles
- 2 tsp. cooking oil
- ½ tsp. bottled minced garlic (1 clove)
- 4 oz. Chinese long beans, cut into 4-inch pieces, or fresh small green beans
- 2 Tbsp. water
- 6 oz. skinless, boneless chicken breast halves, cut into bite-size strips
- ¾ tsp. Thai, Cajun, or other spicy seasoning blend
- 1 medium tomato, cut into wedges
- 1 Tbsp. cider vinegar

fusion chicken

A South American-inspired relish joins forces with a delightful Asian-style sauce in this easy chicken dish.
Makes 4 servings

- ¼ cup water
- 3 Tbsp. hoisin sauce
- 2 Tbsp. peach preserves
- 1 Tbsp. sugar
- 2 tsp. soy sauce
- 2 large oranges
- 3 Tbsp. snipped fresh cilantro
- 4 skinless, boneless chicken breast halves (about 1¼ lb. total)
- 1 Tbsp. cooking oil

shredding peel

Grated citrus peel adds tang to all sorts of dishes. To shred orange, lemon, or lime peel, rub the fruit against a grater with fine holes. Be careful to catch only the colored part of the peel, not the bitter white portion.

chicken, bean, and tomato stir-fry

1. Cook rice noodles in boiling, lightly salted water for 3 to 5 minutes or until tender. Or cook egg noodles according to package directions. Drain noodles. Return to saucepan; cover and keep warm.

2. Meanwhile, pour *1 teaspoon* of the oil into large nonstick skillet; heat over medium-high heat. Add garlic; cook and stir for 15 seconds. Add beans; cook and stir for 2 minutes. Carefully add the water to skillet; reduce heat.

Cover and simmer for 5 to 7 minutes or until beans are crisp-tender. Remove from skillet.

3. Toss chicken with seasoning blend. Add remaining oil to skillet. Add chicken; cook and stir for 3 to 4 minutes or until no longer pink. Stir in noodles, beans, tomato, and vinegar; heat through.

Per Serving: 321 cal., 7 g total fat (1 g sat. fat), 49 mg chol., 284 mg sodium, 44 g carbo., 3 g fiber, 21 g pro.

fusion chicken

1. For sauce, in small bowl, combine the water, hoisin sauce, preserves, sugar, and soy sauce. Finely shred *1 teaspoon* peel from one of the oranges (see tip, above). Stir peel into soy mixture.

2. Peel and section oranges; remove seeds. In small bowl, gently toss oranges and cilantro.

3. In large skillet, cook chicken in hot oil over medium heat for 3 to 5 minutes or until brown, turning once. Drain off fat. Pour sauce mixture

over chicken. Bring to boiling; reduce heat. Cover and simmer for 8 to 10 minutes or until chicken is no longer pink (170°F). Remove chicken from skillet.

4. Boil sauce gently, uncovered, about 5 minutes or until reduced to ⅓ cup. Return chicken to skillet; heat through, turning once to coat with sauce. Serve chicken with orange mixture.

Per Serving: 293 cal., 6 g total fat (1 g sat. fat), 82 mg chol., 369 mg sodium, 24 g carbo., 2 g fiber, 34 g pro.

chicken-feta pitas

This creamy chicken-and-vegetable salad is a tasty way to fill pita bread rounds. Team the sandwiches with a cup of tomato soup and you've got a terrific lunch or light dinner.

Makes 4 servings

turkey scaloppine with peppers

Serrano pepper adds lots of heat to these turkey medallions. For a milder dish, use the Anaheim pepper option.

Makes 4 servings

12	oz. turkey breast tenderloin
½	cup thinly sliced leek
¼	cup thinly sliced red sweet pepper
1	Tbsp. thinly sliced fresh serrano or Anaheim chile pepper (see tip, page 6)
¼	tsp. salt
⅓	cup all-purpose flour
1	Tbsp. cooking oil

chicken-feta pitas

1 9-oz. pkg. frozen chopped cooked chicken, thawed
¾ cup frozen peas, thawed
1 medium tomato, chopped
2 green onions, sliced
¼ cup crumbled feta cheese (1 oz.)
⅓ cup plain fat-free yogurt
1 tsp. dried dillweed
4 pita bread rounds, halved
Torn mixed salad greens

1. In large bowl, combine chicken, peas, tomato, green onion, and feta cheese. Stir in yogurt and dillweed.
2. Line pita halves with salad greens. Fill with chicken mixture. If desired, cut each pita half in half.

Per Serving: 349 cal., 7 g total fat (3 g sat. fat), 63 mg chol., 507 mg sodium, 41 g carbo., 3 g fiber, 28 g pro.

turkey scaloppine with peppers

1. Cut turkey crosswise into four pieces; place each piece between two pieces of plastic wrap. Pound lightly with flat side of meat mallet to ¼-inch thickness; remove plastic wrap.
2. Sprinkle leek, sweet pepper, serrano pepper, and salt on both sides of turkey; cover with plastic wrap. Pound lightly to ⅛-inch thickness; remove plastic wrap. Coat turkey with flour, shaking off any excess.
3. In large heavy skillet, cook turkey in hot oil over medium-high heat for 6 to 8 minutes or until no longer pink, turning once. If desired, serve with lime wedges.

Per Serving: 170 cal., 4 g total fat (1 g sat. fat), 53 mg chol., 179 mg sodium, 10 g carbo., 1 g fiber, 22 g pro.

Test Kitchen Tip: Because hot chile peppers contain volatile oils that can burn your skin and eyes, wear plastic or rubber gloves when handling chile peppers. If skin burns should occur, wash the area well with soapy water. If the juices come in contact with your eyes, flush them with cool water to neutralize the chile pepper oils.

turkey-peach salad

For a light meal, try this fresh-tasting pairing of turkey breast and fruit—topped off with a sprightly onion-and-poppy-seed dressing.

Makes 4 servings

- 2   turkey breast tenderloins (about 1 lb. total)
- 1   tsp. olive oil
- 2   peaches, pitted and sliced
- 2   plums, pitted and sliced
- 2   Tbsp. lemon juice
- ½   cup lemon low-fat yogurt
- 2   Tbsp. thinly sliced green onion
- ¼   tsp. poppy seeds
- Torn mixed salad greens

caribbean chicken *(see photo, page 9)*

This tropical stir-fry starts with work-saving chicken breast tenders, so you can have it ready in next to no time.

Makes 4 servings

- 12   oz. chicken breast tenders
- ¼   tsp. salt
- ⅛   to ¼ tsp. cayenne pepper
- 1   tsp. cooking oil
- 1   medium sweet potato, peeled, halved lengthwise, and thinly sliced

- 1   small fresh banana chile pepper, seeded and chopped
- ¾   cup unsweetened pineapple juice
- 1   tsp. cornstarch
- 2   unripe bananas, quartered lengthwise and cut into ¾-inch pieces

turkey-peach salad

1. Split each turkey tenderloin in half horizontally. Rub both sides of each turkey portion with oil; sprinkle with *salt* and coarsely ground *black pepper.* Place turkey on rack of uncovered grill directly over medium coals. Grill for 12 to 15 minutes or until no longer pink (170°F), turning once. Cut into bite-size pieces.

2. In medium bowl, combine peaches and plums. Add lemon juice; toss gently to coat. For dressing, in small bowl, combine yogurt, green onion, and poppy seeds. If necessary, stir in 1 to 2 teaspoons additional lemon juice to reach drizzling consistency.

3. Divide salad greens among dinner plates. Arrange turkey and fruit on greens. Drizzle with dressing.

Per Serving: 219 cal., 3 g total fat (1 g sat. fat), 70 mg chol., 155 mg sodium, 17 g carbo., 2 g fiber, 30 g pro.

caribbean chicken

1. Sprinkle chicken with salt and cayenne pepper. In large nonstick skillet, cook chicken in hot oil for 3 minutes. Add sweet potato and banana pepper. Cook and stir for 5 to 6 minutes more or until chicken is no longer pink and sweet potato is tender.

2. In small bowl, combine pineapple juice and cornstarch; add to chicken mixture. Cook, stirring gently, until thickened and bubbly. Add banana; cook and stir for 2 minutes more. If desired, serve with hot cooked rice.

Per Serving: 251 cal., 3 g total fat (1 g sat. fat), 49 mg chol., 200 mg sodium, 35 g carbo., 3 g fiber, 22 g pro.

caribbean chicken *(see recipe, page 7)*

snappy
fish &
seafood

grilled salmon tacos

Calling on low-calorie, low-fat fish and seafood is a tasty way to create healthful meals for your family. Try these ideas for everything from salmon to halibut to shrimp.

grilled salmon tacos *(see photo, opposite)*

If you like dishes with plenty of firepower, use chipotle chili powder instead of regular chili powder. It adds smoky flavor along with extra hotness.

Makes 12 to 16 servings

- 1 lb. fresh or frozen skinless salmon fillets
- 8 oz. medium round red or white potatoes, cubed
- 1½ tsp. chili powder or chipotle chili powder
- ¾ tsp. sugar
- ½ tsp. salt
- 1 cup green salsa
- 3 Tbsp. lime juice
- 6 green onions, thinly sliced
- ½ cup snipped fresh cilantro
- 12 6-inch or sixteen 4-inch corn tortillas, warmed
- ½ cup crème fraîche or dairy sour cream
  Lime wedges

pineapple-glazed orange roughy

All it takes is pineapple preserves, a splash of vinegar, and a few seasonings to dress up orange roughy in this fix-in-a-flash recipe.

Makes 4 servings

- 1 lb. fresh or frozen orange roughy fillets
- 3 Tbsp. pineapple preserves
- 2 Tbsp. rice vinegar
- 2 tsp. snipped fresh thyme
- ½ tsp. bottled minced garlic
- ⅛ tsp. crushed red pepper
- ¼ tsp. ground black pepper
- ⅛ tsp. salt

grilled salmon tacos

1. Thaw fish, if frozen. In covered small saucepan, cook potatoes in enough boiling salted water to cover about 15 minutes or until tender. Drain and cool.

2. In small bowl, combine chili powder, sugar, and ¼ *teaspoon* of the salt. Rinse fish; pat dry. Measure thickness of fish. Rub chili powder mixture into fish. Place fish on greased rack of uncovered grill directly over medium coals. Grill for 4 to 6 minutes per ½-inch thickness or until fish flakes easily with a fork, turning once. Cool slightly. Break fish into chunks.

3. In medium bowl, stir together salsa, lime juice, and remaining salt. Add potatoes, fish, green onion, and cilantro; toss gently to coat.

4. Divide fish mixture among tortillas. Top with crème fraîche; fold tortillas. Serve with lime wedges.

Per Serving: 161 cal., 5 g total fat (2 g sat. fat), 29 mg chol., 316 mg sodium, 19 g carbo., 2 g fiber, 10 g pro.

pineapple-glazed orange roughy

1. Thaw fish, if frozen. Preheat broiler. In small bowl, stir together preserves, vinegar, thyme, garlic, and crushed red pepper.

2. Rinse fish; pat dry. Measure thickness of fish. Cut into four serving-size pieces. Sprinkle fish with black pepper and salt.

3. Place fish on greased unheated rack of broiler pan. Broil 4 inches from heat for 4 to 6 minutes per ½-inch thickness or until fish flakes easily with a fork, brushing occasionally with preserves mixture the last half of broiling. (If fish is 1 inch or more thick, turn once.)

Per Serving: 125 cal., 1 g total fat (0 g sat. fat), 22 mg chol., 150 mg sodium, 11 g carbo., 0 g fiber, 17 g pro.

shrimp kabobs

Tailor these kabobs to fit folks with differing tastes. For those who like their foods fiery, use a knock-your-socks-off barbecue sauce; for mild barbecue fans, slather on a less intense version.

Makes 4 servings

1	lb. fresh or frozen medium to large shrimp in shells
1	small red or green sweet pepper, cut into 16 pieces
¼	of a medium fresh pineapple, cut into chunks
4	green onions, cut into 1-inch pieces
¼	cup barbecue sauce

smoked salmon club sandwich (see photo, page 15)

While this fish-style version of the traditional club sandwich may be short on calories and fat, it's definitely not short on flavor—chives and cayenne pepper give it plenty of zip.

Makes 8 servings

½	of an 8-oz. pkg. reduced-fat cream cheese (Neufchâtel), softened
1	small red or yellow sweet pepper, very finely chopped
1	small zucchini, very finely chopped
1	small carrot, very finely chopped
2	Tbsp. snipped fresh chives
	Cayenne pepper
12	slices sesame sourdough bread
2	Tbsp. light dairy sour cream
6	oz. thinly sliced smoked salmon
1½	cups fresh baby spinach
1	large cucumber, thinly bias-sliced

shrimp kabobs

1. Thaw shrimp, if frozen. Preheat broiler, if using. Peel and devein shrimp; if desired, leave tails intact. Rinse shrimp; pat dry. On eight metal skewers, alternately thread shrimp, sweet pepper, pineapple, and green onion, leaving ¼ inch between pieces.

2. Place skewers on greased unheated rack of broiler pan. Broil 4 inches from heat for 8 to 10 minutes or until shrimp are opaque, turning skewers and brushing once with barbecue sauce. (Or place skewers on greased rack of uncovered grill directly over medium coals. Grill for 6 to 8 minutes or until shrimp are opaque, turning skewers and brushing once with barbecue sauce.)

Per Serving: 134 cal., 2 g total fat (0 g sat. fat), 129 mg chol., 258 mg sodium, 10 g carbo., 1 g fiber, 18 g pro.

smoked salmon club sandwich

1. For vegetable spread, in medium bowl, stir together cream cheese, sweet pepper, zucchini, carrot, and chives. Season to taste with cayenne pepper and *salt.* If desired, cover and chill for 1 to 24 hours.

2. To assemble, spread *four slices* of the bread with sour cream. Arrange salmon on sour cream; add spinach. Spread additional *four slices* of the bread with vegetable spread; set on sandwich bases, spread sides up. Place cucumber on vegetable spread. Top with remaining slices of the bread. Cut sandwiches into quarters.

Per Serving: 181 cal., 6 g total fat (3 g sat. fat), 17 mg chol., 501 mg sodium, 23 g carbo., 2 g fiber, 10 g pro.

smoked salmon club sandwich
(see recipe, page 13)

pork & beef
express

pork medallions with cran-fig chutney

Hungry for something different for dinner tonight? You've come to the right place. Choose one of these timesaving entrées. Each is a standout.

pork medallions with cran-fig chutney *(see photo, opposite)*

This ruby-red chutney is the perfect flavor match for pan-fried pork. Try the relish with broiled or grilled boneless chicken breast halves too.

Makes 2 servings

½	cup fresh or frozen cranberries
¼	cup apple juice
2	Tbsp. snipped dried figs
1	Tbsp. packed brown sugar
¼	tsp. dried rosemary, crushed
6	oz. pork tenderloin
2	tsp. cooking oil

pork with berry-dressed greens

Makes 4 servings

2	boneless pork loin chops, cut ¾ inch thick
¼	tsp. salt
¼	tsp. ground ginger
⅛	tsp. ground black pepper
1	tsp. cooking oil
1	tsp. bottled minced garlic
½	cup sugar snap peas
⅓	cup sliced fresh mushrooms
⅔	cup reduced-fat raspberry vinaigrette salad dressing
½	cup raspberries
8	cups torn mixed salad greens

coming clean A foolproof way to wash greens is to remove and discard any discolored or wilted leaves. Rinse the greens under cold running water and drain them in a colander. Then place them on a clean kitchen towel or several layers of paper towels and pat dry.

pork medallions with cran-fig chutney

1. For chutney, in small heavy saucepan, combine cranberries, apple juice, figs, brown sugar, and rosemary. Bring to boiling; reduce heat. Simmer, uncovered, for 5 to 8 minutes or until desired consistency, stirring occasionally. Season to taste with *salt* and ground *black pepper.*

2. Meanwhile, trim fat from meat. Cut meat crosswise into six slices. Press with palm of hand to even 1/4-inch thickness. In large nonstick skillet, cook meat in hot oil over medium-high heat for 2 to 3 minutes or until slightly pink in center, turning once.

3. To serve, arrange meat on dinner plates. Spoon some of the chutney over meat. Pass remaining chutney.

Per Serving: 227 cal., 7 g total fat (1 g sat. fat), 55 mg chol., 185 mg sodium, 23 g carbo., 3 g fiber, 18 g pro.

pork with berry-dressed greens

1. Trim fat from meat. Sprinkle both sides of meat with salt, ginger, and pepper. In large nonstick skillet, cook meat in hot oil over medium heat for 8 to 12 minutes or until juices run clear (160°F), turning once. Remove from skillet, reserving drippings. Cover meat; keep warm.

2. In same skillet, cook and stir garlic in reserved drippings for 30 seconds. Add snap peas and mushrooms; pour vinaigrette over vegetables. Cover and cook for 2 to 3 minutes or until heated through. Remove from heat. Gently stir in raspberries; cover and keep warm.

3. Divide salad greens among dinner plates. Thinly slice meat; arrange meat on greens. Pour raspberry mixture over salads.

Per Serving: 248 cal., 12 g total fat (2 g sat. fat), 46 mg chol., 617 mg sodium, 12 g carbo., 7 g fiber, 21 g pro.

peppercorn steaks

Just a touch of mild molasses adds a distinctive rich flavor to the beef, sugar snap peas, and carrots.

Makes 4 servings

2	6-oz. beef ribeye steaks, cut 1 inch thick
1	Tbsp. multicolored peppercorns, crushed
2	Tbsp. butter, softened
2	tsp. mild-flavored molasses
1/4	tsp. finely shredded lemon peel
1	tsp. lemon juice
2	cups sugar snap peas
1/2	cup carrot cut into thin bite-size strips

beef-asparagus sauté *(see photo, page 21)*

An herbed Marsala sauce adds a note of sophistication to this quick-fixing sauté. Marsala wine can be sweet, semisweet, or dry. The dry variety is best for accenting this dish.

Makes 4 servings

12	oz. asparagus spears
1	lb. boneless beef sirloin or tenderloin
2	tsp. olive oil
1	small carrot, shredded
1	tsp. dried herbes de Provence or basil, crushed
1/2	cup dry Marsala
1/4	tsp. finely shredded lemon peel

peppercorn steaks

1. Preheat broiler. Trim fat from meat. Press peppercorns and 1/2 teaspoon *salt* into both sides of meat. Place meat on unheated rack of broiler pan. Broil 3 to 4 inches from heat until desired doneness, turning once. Allow 12 to 14 minutes for medium-rare (145°F) or 15 to 18 minutes for medium (160°F).

2. Meanwhile, in small bowl, combine butter, molasses, lemon peel, and lemon juice (mixture will appear curdled).

3. In covered medium saucepan, cook snap peas and carrot in small amount of boiling salted water for 2 to 4 minutes or until crisp-tender; drain. Stir in *1 tablespoon* of the molasses mixture.

4. To serve, top meat with remaining molasses mixture. Thinly slice meat; toss with vegetable mixture. If desired, garnish with lemon peel strips.

Per Serving: 247 cal., 12 g total fat (6 g sat. fat), 66 mg chol., 418 mg sodium, 13 g carbo., 3 g fiber, 20 g pro.

beef-asparagus sauté

1. Snap off and discard woody bases from asparagus. Bias-slice asparagus into 2-inch pieces. Trim fat from meat. Thinly slice meat across the grain into bite-size strips. Sprinkle with *salt* and ground *black pepper.*

2. Pour oil into large nonstick skillet; heat over medium-high heat. Add meat; cook and stir for 2 minutes. Add asparagus, carrot, and herbes de Provence; cook and stir for 2 minutes more. Stir in Marsala and lemon peel; reduce heat.

3. Cook for 2 to 3 minutes or until asparagus is crisp-tender, stirring occasionally. If desired, serve with hot cooked rice

Per Serving: 207 cal., 8 g total fat (2 g sat. fat), 69 mg chol., 67 mg sodium, 2 g carbo., 1 g fiber, 26 g pro.

beef-asparagus sauté (see recipe, page 19)

meatless
tonight

herbed pasta primavera

Whether you're trying to follow a strict vegetarian meal plan or enjoy only an occasional meatless meal, you'll find creative dishes here to spark your appetite.

herbed pasta primavera *(see photo, opposite)*

A nice selection of fresh vegetables makes this lively primavera just the ticket for a light dinner or lunch.

Makes 4 servings

6	oz. dried penne pasta
1	cup water
1	Tbsp. cornstarch
2	tsp. instant chicken bouillon granules
8	oz. tiny whole carrots with tops (about 12)
1½	cups green beans bias-sliced into 2-inch pieces
2	medium leeks, halved lengthwise and cut into ¼-inch slices
½	tsp. bottled minced garlic (1 clove)
8	oz. baby pattypan squash
1	tsp. dried basil, crushed
½	tsp. dried dillweed
¼	cup slivered almonds, toasted

spaghetti with vegetarian sauce bolognese

In this adaptation of traditional Italian Bolognese meat sauce, cereal creates a chewy texture that is remarkably similar to that of ground meat. Be sure to serve the sauce immediately.

Makes 4 servings

6	oz. dried spaghetti
½	cup finely chopped carrot
½	cup thinly sliced celery
1	medium onion, finely chopped
1½	tsp. bottled minced garlic (3 cloves)
½	tsp. dried oregano, crushed
¼	tsp. salt
¼	tsp. ground black pepper
1	Tbsp. olive oil
1	14½-oz. can low-sodium stewed tomatoes with onion, celery, and green peppers, undrained and cut up
1	8-oz. can tomato sauce
¼	cup water
¾	cup Grape Nuts cereal
	Grated Parmesan cheese (optional)

toasting nuts

Toasting nuts and seeds gives them a fuller flavor. To toast, spread the nuts or seeds in a single layer in a shallow baking pan. Bake in a 350°F oven for 5 to 10 minutes or until golden, stirring once or twice to prevent burning.

- -

herbed pasta primavera

1. Cook pasta according to package directions; drain. Return to saucepan; cover and keep warm.

2. Meanwhile, for sauce, in small bowl, combine the water, cornstarch, and bouillon granules. If desired, cut off tops of carrots. Cut carrots in half lengthwise.

3. Lightly coat wok or large skillet with *nonstick cooking spray;* heat over medium-high heat. Add carrots; cook and stir for 5 minutes. Add green beans, leek, and garlic; cook and stir for 2 minutes more. Stir in squash and 2 tablespoons *water.* Cover and cook for 3 to 4 minutes or until vegetables are crisp-tender. Push from center of wok.

4. Stir sauce; add to wok. Cook and stir until thickened and bubbly. Add basil and dillweed; stir all ingredients together. Cook and stir for 1 to 2 minutes more or until heated through. Spoon vegetable mixture over pasta. Sprinkle with almonds.

Per Serving: 272 cal., 5 g total fat (10 g sat. fat), 0 mg chol., 518 mg sodium, 48 g carbo., 7 g fiber, 10 g pro.

- -

spaghetti with vegetarian sauce bolognese

1. Cook spaghetti according to package directions; drain. Return to saucepan; cover and keep warm.

2. Meanwhile, in medium saucepan, cook carrot, celery, onion, garlic, oregano, salt, and pepper in hot oil over medium-high heat about 5 minutes or until onion is tender. Stir in tomatoes, tomato sauce, and the water. Bring to boiling; reduce heat.

Cover and simmer for 5 minutes. Stir in cereal; return to boiling. Remove from heat.

3. Divide pasta among dinner plates. Top with tomato mixture. If desired, sprinkle with Parmesan cheese.

Per Serving: 329 cal., 5 g total fat (1 g sat. fat), 0 mg chol., 677 mg sodium, 66 g carbo., 6 g fiber, 10 g pro.

barley-stuffed peppers *(see photo, page 27)*

These aren't your grandmother's stuffed peppers—they feature a newfangled herbed filling of fresh vegetables, cheese, and barley.

Makes 4 servings

- 1 cup sliced fresh mushrooms
- 1 cup vegetable broth
- ⅔ cup quick-cooking barley
- 2 large red, yellow, and/or orange sweet peppers
- 1 egg, beaten
- 1 large tomato, seeded and chopped
- ½ cup bias-sliced small green beans
- ¼ cup finely shredded Parmesan cheese (1 oz.)
- 3 Tbsp. fine dry bread crumbs
- ½ tsp. dried basil, crushed
- ¼ tsp. dried rosemary, crushed
- ⅛ tsp. salt
- ⅛ tsp. crushed red pepper
  Finely shredded Parmesan cheese (optional)

beans, barley, and tomatoes

Edamame is the Japanese name for green soybeans. They serve as a scrumptious counterpoint to barley in this hearty dish. Look for edamame in Asian food or health food stores.

Makes 4 servings

barley-stuffed peppers

1. In medium saucepan, combine mushrooms, broth, and barley. Bring to boiling; reduce heat. Cover and simmer for 10 to 12 minutes or until barley is tender. If necessary, drain.

2. Cut sweet peppers in half lengthwise; remove seeds and membranes. Precook peppers in boiling water for 1 to 3 minutes. Invert onto paper towels to drain.

3. In medium bowl, combine egg, tomato, green beans, cheese, bread crumbs, basil, rosemary, salt, and crushed red pepper. Stir in barley mixture. Place peppers, cut sides up, in 2-quart rectangular baking dish. Fill with barley mixture.

4. Cover and bake in 350°F oven for 25 to 35 minutes or until filling is heated through. If desired, sprinkle with additional cheese.

Per Serving: 184 cal., 4 g total fat (2 g sat. fat), 59 mg chol., 395 mg sodium, 30 g carbo., 5 g fiber, 9 g pro.

beans, barley, and tomatoes

1	14-oz. can vegetable broth
1	tsp. Greek seasoning or garam masala
1	cup frozen green soybeans (shelled edamame)
¾	cup quick-cooking barley
½	cup shredded carrot
4	cups fresh spinach leaves
4	small to medium tomatoes, sliced

1. In medium saucepan, bring broth and Greek seasoning to boiling. Stir in soybeans and barley. Return to boiling; reduce heat. Cover and simmer for 10 to 12 minutes or until barley is tender. Stir in carrot.

2. Meanwhile, divide spinach among dinner plates. Arrange tomato on spinach. Drain barley mixture; spoon over tomato.

Per Serving: 171 cal., 3 g total fat (0 g sat. fat), 0 mg chol., 484 mg sodium, 33 g carbo., 10 g fiber, 9 g pro.

barley-stuffed peppers (see recipe, page 25)

sensational sides

curly cukes and radish salad

When grilling steak or chicken for dinner, complete the menu with one of these refreshing salads, rice dishes, or vegetable sides.

curly cukes and radish salad *(see photo, opposite)*

To add interest to this lively quick-fixing salad, use a mixture of traditional round radishes and the longer watermelon radishes.

Makes 6 servings

10	radishes
2	medium seedless cucumbers
2	Tbsp. coarsely snipped fresh basil
1	fresh jalapeño chile pepper, seeded and sliced (see tip, page 6)
½	tsp. sugar
¼	tsp. salt
1	Tbsp. olive oil
1	Tbsp. white wine vinegar

baby carrots with pistachios

You won't have trouble getting the family to eat veggies when you serve these lemon- and cardamom-accented carrots dusted with pistachios.

Makes 4 to 6 servings

1¼	lb. small whole carrots with tops or 1 lb. carrots
2	Tbsp. lemon juice
¼	tsp. salt
¼	tsp. ground black pepper
⅛	tsp. ground cardamom
1	Tbsp. olive oil
¼	cup coarsely chopped shelled unsalted pistachio nuts

vegetable ribbons

Make attractive ribbons from cucumbers and other firm vegetables by drawing a sharp vegetable peeler lengthwise along the vegetable to cut very thin slices.

curly cukes and radish salad

1. Thinly slice *five* of the radishes. Cut remaining radishes into halves or quarters. Using a vegetable peeler, cut cucumbers lengthwise into thin ribbons (see tip, above). Discard first cucumber slices.

2. In medium bowl, combine radishes, cucumber, basil, jalapeño pepper, sugar, and salt. Drizzle with oil and vinegar; toss gently to coat.

Per Serving: 36 cal., 2 g total fat (0 g sat. fat), 0 mg chol., 93 mg sodium, 4 g carbo., 1 g fiber, 1 g pro.

baby carrots with pistachios

1. Trim tops of small carrots to 1 inch long. Cut long carrots in half lengthwise; halve crosswise.

2. Place steamer basket in large saucepan; add water to just below basket. Bring to boiling. Add carrots to basket; reduce heat. Cover and steam for 7 to 9 minutes or until tender.

3. In small bowl, combine lemon juice, salt, pepper, and cardamom; whisk in oil. Transfer to shallow dish. Add carrots; toss to coat. Cover and marinate in refrigerator for 4 to 24 hours, tossing once or twice.

4. To serve, transfer carrots to serving bowl. Sprinkle with pistachios.

Per Serving: 133 cal., 8 g total fat (1 g sat. fat), 0 mg chol., 188 mg sodium, 15 g carbo., 1 g fiber, 3 g pro.

fruit verde

When it comes to the "wearing of the green," this salad does it deliciously. It features a mint-and-kiwifruit syrup tossed with honeydew melon, green grapes, and pear.

Makes 8 servings

honeydew-apple salad

This salad is a terrific addition to meals during the dog days of summer, when melon and nectarines are at their peak. In the winter, try it with orange sections and banana chunks.

Makes 6 servings

make it mint

Mint adds a cool, sweet note to all types of dishes. Spearmint and peppermint are varieties most commonly sold in supermarkets, but at farmers' markets you also may find apple (shown), lemon, and pineapple varieties.

fruit verde

- 3 **kiwifruits**
- ½ **cup loosely packed fresh mint leaves**
- ½ **cup white grape juice**
- 1 **cup honeydew melon and/or cantaloupe balls or cubes**
- 1 **cup seedless green grapes**
- 1 **pear, cored and cut into ½-inch pieces**

1. For syrup, peel and cut up *one* of the kiwifruits. Place in blender; add mint and grape juice. Cover and blend until smooth. Cover and chill for at least 1 hour.

2. Meanwhile, in large bowl, combine melon, grapes, and pear. Peel and thinly slice remaining kiwifruits; gently stir into melon mixture. Cover and chill.

3. To serve, pour syrup over fruit; toss gently to coat.

Per Serving: 68 cal., 0 g total fat, 0 mg chol., 4 mg sodium, 16 g carbo., 1 g fiber, 1 g pro.

honeydew-apple salad

- ½ **of a medium honeydew melon, peeled, seeded, and cut into bite-size pieces (2 cups)**
- 2 **medium tart apples, cored and cut into bite-size pieces**
- 2 **medium nectarines, pitted and thinly sliced**
- ¼ **cup vanilla low-fat yogurt**
- 3 **Tbsp. apricot jam**
- ¼ **tsp. ground ginger**
- 1 **cup red raspberries**

1. In large bowl, combine melon, apple, and nectarine. For dressing, in small bowl, stir together yogurt, jam, and ginger.

2. Pour dressing over fruit mixture; toss gently to coat. Spoon into dishes. Top with raspberries.

Per Serving: 109 cal., 1 g total fat (0 g sat. fat), 1 mg chol., 16 mg sodium, 27 g carbo., 3 g fiber, 1 g pro.

lemony oven fries

Wow! A zap of lemon gives these oven-baked french fries a surprising burst of fresh tangy flavor.

Makes 10 servings

- ⅓ **cup olive oil**
- 1 **large lemon, thinly sliced**
- ¼ **cup fresh flat-leaf parsley sprigs**
- 1 **20-oz. pkg. frozen french-fried shoestring potatoes**
  Coarse sea salt
  Lemon wedges

mustard-curry potato salad *(see photo, page 35)*

This intriguing East Indian version of potato salad is just what you need to add interest to a simple meal of grilled or broiled beef, pork, or chicken.

Makes 8 to 10 servings

- 2 **lb. tiny new potatoes (about 24 potatoes), halved**
- 2 **cups coarsely shredded cabbage**
- ⅓ **cup olive oil**
- 1 **Tbsp. curry powder**
- 3 **Tbsp. vinegar**
- 1 **Tbsp. coarse-grain brown mustard**
- 1 **tsp. salt**
- ½ **tsp. coarsely ground black pepper**
- ¾ **cup sliced celery**

lemony oven fries

1. In large skillet, heat oil over medium heat. Carefully add lemon slices; cook for 3 to 5 minutes or until lemon starts to brown. Turn lemon slices; add parsley. Cook for 20 to 30 seconds more or until parsley is crisp. Using slotted spoon, remove lemon and parsley; drain on paper towels. Reserve lemon-flavored oil (should have about 3 tablespoons).
2. In large bowl, drizzle reserved lemon-flavored oil over potatoes; toss gently to coat. Transfer potatoes to 15×10×1-inch baking pan. Bake according to package directions or until browned and crisp, stirring occasionally.
3. To serve, add lemon slices and parsley to potatoes; toss gently to combine. Sprinkle generously with sea salt. Squeeze lemon wedges over fries.

Per Serving: 126 cal., 7 g total fat (1 g sat. fat), 0 mg chol., 72 mg sodium, 14 g carbo., 1 g fiber, 2 g pro.

mustard-curry potato salad

1. In covered Dutch oven, cook potato in small amount of boiling salted water for 12 to 15 minutes or just until tender, adding cabbage the last 1 to 2 minutes; drain. Cool slightly.
2. For dressing, in medium skillet, heat oil over medium heat. Add curry powder; cook and stir for 1 minute. Carefully stir in vinegar, mustard, salt, and pepper. Cool slightly.
3. In large bowl, combine potato mixture and celery. Add dressing; toss gently to coat.

Per Serving: 133 cal., 9 g total fat (1 g sat. fat), 0 mg chol., 588 mg sodium, 12 g carbo., 2 g fiber, 1 g pro.

mustard-curry potato salad (see recipe, page 33)

cool
snacks

dried cranberry chutney appetizers

Check out these flavor-packed ideas and you're sure to find just the right nibble to serve at your next party or to cure an attack of between-meal hunger pangs.

dried cranberry chutney
appetizers *(see photo, opposite)*

Mango chutney spruced up with dried cranberries makes a tongue-tingling snack when you spoon it on crackers, apple slices, or French bread slices spread with cream cheese.

Makes 22 servings

½ cup dried cranberries
¼ cup water
2 Tbsp. sugar
1 Tbsp. finely chopped fresh ginger
¾ cup mango chutney
   Cream cheese (optional)
   Crackers, apple slices, and/or toasted baguette slices

cherry bruschetta

To serve these magnificent cherry-and-blue-cheese morsels for a party, toast the French bread ahead and assemble the stacks just before guests arrive.

Makes 12 servings

pitting cherries Make easy work of removing the pits from fresh cherries for Cherry Bruschetta by using a cherry pitter. Place the fruit, stem end up, in the gadget as shown and squeeze out the pit.

dried cranberry chutney appetizers

1. In small saucepan, combine dried cranberries, the water, sugar, and ginger. Bring to boiling. Cover and remove from heat. Let stand for 15 minutes.

2. Snip any large pieces of chutney. Stir chutney into cranberry mixture. Cover and chill for at least 2 hours.

3. If desired, spread cream cheese on crackers, apples, and/or baguette slices. Top with chutney mixture.

Per Serving: 37 cal., 0 g total fat, 0 mg chol., 2 mg sodium, 9 g carbo., 0 g fiber, 0 g pro.

cherry bruschetta

2 **cups coarsely chopped pitted sweet cherries**

¼ **cup jalapeño pepper jelly**

24 **½-inch slices French bread, toasted**

¼ **cup crumbled blue cheese (1 oz.)**

2 **to 3 Tbsp. slivered almonds**

1. In small bowl, combine cherries and jalapeño jelly. Spoon cherry mixture onto bread slices.

2. Sprinkle with blue cheese and slivered almonds.

Per Serving: 53 cal., 1 g total fat (0 g sat. fat), 2 mg chol., 35 mg sodium, 9 g carbo., 1 g fiber, 1 g pro.

baked vegetable dippers

Makes 8 servings

- ¾ cup cornflake crumbs
- 2 Tbsp. grated Romano cheese
- ⅛ tsp. garlic powder
- ⅛ tsp. cayenne pepper
- 2 egg whites
- 2 Tbsp. water
- 2 small zucchini and/or yellow summer squash, cut into ¼-inch slices
- 1 cup cauliflower florets
- 1 cup broccoli florets or halved small fresh mushrooms
- 1 8-oz. can pizza sauce, warmed

texas-style quesadillas

Although quesadillas are generally made with flour tortillas, this version showcases white corn tortillas. Look for them at Mexican food stores.

Makes 6 servings

storing cilantro To store a bunch of fresh cilantro, snip off the ends of the stems and discard any withered leaves. Then rinse the bunch under cold running water and shake off as much water as possible. Place the stems in a glass with about 2 inches of water. Cover the leaves loosely with a plastic bag and refrigerate.

baked vegetable dippers

1. Preheat oven to 400°F. In small bowl, combine cornflake crumbs, cheese, garlic powder, and cayenne pepper. In another small bowl, beat together egg whites and the water.

2. Dip zucchini, cauliflower, and broccoli into egg white mixture; roll in crumb mixture to coat. Place in single layer on greased baking sheet. Bake for 8 to 10 minutes or until crumb coating is golden.

3. Serve vegetable dippers with warm pizza sauce.

Per Serving: 51 cal., 1 g total fat (0 g sat. fat), 1 mg chol., 232 mg sodium, 9 g carbo., 1 g fiber, 3 g pro.

texas-style quesadillas

6   4-inch or four 6-inch white corn tortillas
    Cooking oil or nonstick cooking spray
½   cup shredded Monterey Jack cheese (2 oz.)
1   roma tomato, chopped
2   to 3 fresh serrano chile peppers, seeded and thinly sliced (see tip, page 6)
2   Tbsp. snipped fresh cilantro
2   Tbsp. light dairy sour cream

1. Lightly brush one side of tortillas with oil or lightly coat with cooking spray. Divide cheese among unoiled sides of *half* of the tortillas. Add tomato, serrano pepper, and cilantro. Top with remaining tortillas, oiled sides up.

2. Heat heavy skillet or griddle over medium heat. Cook quesadillas, one at a time, for 2 to 4 minutes or until cheese melts and tortillas are lightly browned, turning once. Cut into wedges. Serve with sour cream.

Per Serving: 105 cal., 5 g total fat (2 g sat. fat), 10 mg chol., 57 mg sodium, 11 g carbo., 1 g fiber, 4 g pro.

herbed candied strawberries

The sweet rosemary flavor of the berries is a tantalizing match for the tangy flavor of goat cheese. If you like, serve the candied fruit as a relish with lamb or pork chops, chicken, or ham.

Makes 2 cups (16 to 20 servings)

seafood bruschetta *(see photo, page 43)*

This is no ordinary bruschetta. This take on the traditional tomato-and-herb topping includes a touch of mint as well as shrimp and crabmeat.

Makes 48 servings

3	Tbsp. olive oil
1	Tbsp. snipped fresh chives
1	Tbsp. snipped fresh basil
1	Tbsp. snipped fresh mint
1	Tbsp. lemon juice
1	tsp. bottled minced garlic (2 cloves)

8 oz. peeled and deveined cooked shrimp, coarsely chopped

6 oz. cooked crabmeat, coarsely chopped; or one 6$\frac{1}{2}$-oz. can crabmeat, drained, flaked, and cartilage removed

1 cup chopped roma tomato

$\frac{1}{2}$ cup finely chopped onion

1 8-oz. loaf baguette-style French bread

herbed candied strawberries

2 **Tbsp. strawberry or apple jelly**
4 **tsp. finely chopped crystallized ginger**
1 **Tbsp. lemon juice**
2 **cups strawberries, stemmed and halved**
1 **Tbsp. snipped fresh rosemary**
  Goat cheese (chèvre), thinly sliced
  Toasted baguette slices

1. In medium microwave-safe bowl, combine jelly, crystallized ginger, and lemon juice. Microwave on 100 percent power (high) for 30 to 60 seconds or just until jelly is melted. Stir in strawberries and rosemary.

2. For each serving, place *one slice* of cheese on *each* baguette slice. Top with *one or two* of the candied berries.

Per Serving: 72 cal., 2 g total fat (1 g sat. fat), 4 mg chol., 110 mg sodium, 10 g carbo., 1 g fiber, 3 g pro.

seafood bruschetta

1. Preheat broiler. In medium bowl, stir together *1 tablespoon* of the olive oil, the chives, basil, mint, lemon juice, and garlic. Add shrimp, crabmeat, tomato, and onion; toss gently to coat.

2. Cut bread into 48 thin slices. Arrange on large baking sheet. Brush with remaining olive oil; sprinkle lightly with freshly ground *black pepper.* Broil 3 to 4 inches from heat for 2 to 3 minutes or until toasted, turning once.

3. To serve, spoon seafood mixture onto oiled sides of bread.

Per Serving: 32 cal., 1 g total fat (0 g sat. fat), 13 mg chol., 48 mg sodium, 3 g carbo., 0 g fiber, 2 g pro.

seafood bruschetta (see recipe, page 41)

guilt-free
desserts

berry trifle

Just because you're watching what you eat doesn't mean desserts are off-limits. These luscious but healthful tempters are a sure bet to satisfy your sweet tooth.

berry trifle *(see photo, opposite)*

If you prefer a nonalcoholic version of this spectacular dessert, substitute bottled raspberry syrup for the raspberry liqueur.

Makes 4 servings

½ of a 3-oz. pkg. ladyfingers (12 halves), cubed
4 tsp. raspberry liqueur
1½ cups raspberries, blueberries, and/or sliced strawberries
1 cup cubed red and/or yellow papaya
1 8-oz. carton vanilla low-fat yogurt
¼ of an 8-oz. container frozen fat-free whipped dessert topping, thawed

mango parfaits

Mango cubes tossed with orange liqueur and layered with a vanilla cream make for a tasty low-calorie treat. Serve this tropical delight with coconut macaroons on the side.

Makes 4 servings

½ of an 8-oz. container frozen light whipped dessert topping, thawed
½ cup light dairy sour cream
1 tsp. vanilla
3 medium ripe mangoes
1 Tbsp. orange liqueur or orange juice

cubing mango

To easily cube mango, first slice an unpeeled mango down both sides of the seed. Then make a series of crosshatch cuts in each half of the fruit and push the fruit "inside out." You should be able to easily remove the pieces with a knife.

berry trifle

1. Divide cubed ladyfingers among four dessert dishes. Drizzle with raspberry liqueur. Top with *half* of the berries and *half* of the papaya.

2. In small bowl, fold together yogurt and whipped topping. Spoon over fruit mixture. Top with remaining berries and papaya.

Per Serving: 165 cal., 2 g total fat (1 g sat. fat), 42 mg chol., 63 mg sodium, 30 g carbo., 3 g fiber, 4 g pro.

mango parfaits

1. In medium bowl, fold together whipped topping, sour cream, and vanilla. If desired, cover and chill.

2. Seed and peel mangoes; cut into $1/2$-inch cubes (see tip, above). In medium bowl, combine mango and orange liqueur; toss gently to coat. Alternately layer mango cubes and sour cream mixture in parfait or wine glasses.

Per Serving: 217 cal., 6 g total fat (5 g sat. fat), 10 mg chol., 23 mg sodium, 36 g carbo., 3 g fiber, 3 g pro.

jelly-roll dainties

Take your choice of fruit preserves, lemon curd, or prepared pudding to fill these delicate mini cake rolls.

Makes 12 servings

- ¼ cup all-purpose flour
- ½ tsp. baking powder
- 2 egg yolks
- ¼ tsp. vanilla
- 6 Tbsp. granulated sugar
- 2 egg whites
  Sifted powdered sugar
- ⅓ to ⅔ cup fruit preserves, lemon curd, and/or prepared pudding

chocolate-orange custard

For the best flavor, make this intensely fudgy dessert with a high-quality chocolate. If you like, garnish the desserts with chocolate shavings and kumquat slices or berries.

Makes 4 servings

- Sugar
- 1¼ cups milk
- 2 oz. semisweet chocolate, coarsely chopped
- 3 Tbsp. sugar
- 3 eggs, beaten
- 1 tsp. vanilla
- ½ tsp. orange extract

jelly-roll dainties

1. Preheat oven to 350°F. Grease 15×10×1-inch jelly-roll pan. Line bottom with waxed paper; grease paper. Stir together flour and baking powder.

2. Beat egg yolks and vanilla with electric mixer on high speed about 5 minutes or until thickened. Slowly add *3 tablespoons* of the granulated sugar, beating until sugar dissolves.

3. Wash beaters. Beat egg whites on medium speed until soft peaks form. Slowly add remaining granulated sugar, beating until stiff peaks form. Fold in yolk mixture. Gently fold in flour mixture. Spread in prepared pan.

4. Bake for 8 to 10 minutes or until cake springs back when lightly touched. Immediately turn out onto towel sprinkled with powdered sugar. Peel off paper. Starting from short side, roll up towel and cake jelly-roll style. Cool on wire rack for at least 1 hour.

5. Unroll cake; remove towel. Cut cake in half lengthwise; cut each half into thirds. Spread with preserves. Roll up; cut in half. If desired, sprinkle with additional powdered sugar.

Per Serving: 70 cal., 1 g total fat (0 g sat. fat), 35 mg chol., 30 mg sodium, 14 g carbo., 0 g fiber, 1 g pro.

chocolate-orange custard

1. Preheat oven to 325°F. Butter bottoms and 1 inch up sides of four 6-ounce ovenproof star molds or custard cups; sprinkle lightly with sugar. Place prepared molds in shallow baking dish. In medium saucepan, combine milk, chocolate, and the 3 tablespoons sugar. Cook and stir over medium heat until chocolate melts. In medium bowl, combine eggs, vanilla, and orange extract. Slowly whisk chocolate mixture into egg mixture; skim off any foam.

2. Place baking dish on oven rack. Pour egg mixture into molds. Pour boiling water into baking dish around molds to a depth of 1 inch.

3. Bake for 25 to 35 minutes or until knife inserted near centers comes out clean. Remove custards from baking dish; cool on wire rack. Cover and chill. To serve, unmold custards onto dessert plates.

Per Serving: 215 cal., 10 g total fat (5 g sat. fat), 167 mg chol., 91 mg sodium, 22 g carbo., 1 g fiber, 8 g pro.